Max and little plant

Story by Annette Smith
Illustrations by Richard Hoit

DISCARD

Paradise Valley/Machado Media Center
Morgan Hill Unified School District

Max liked helping Grandpa in the garden.

"You are good at helping me in the garden, Max," said Grandpa. "Here is a little plant for you. It can go in here."

Max looked after
his little plant,
and it got bigger and bigger.

One hot day,
Max went to look
at his plant.

"Oh, no!" he said.
"It is very hot today,
and I forgot
to water my plant."

"My plant is too dry,"
said Max.

He ran to get some water
for it.

"Grandpa!

Come and look at my plant!"

shouted Max.

"It liked the water.

It is sitting up again!"

The plant got bigger
and bigger,
day after day.

"Look up here, Max,"
said Grandpa.
"Your plant is going to flower."

"The flower is yellow!" said Max.

"My plant is a sunflower."